Wacky Sentences Handwriting Workbook (Reproducible)

Practice Writing in Cursive (Third and Fourth Grade)

by Julie Harper

Wacky Sentences Handwriting Workbook (Reproducible): Practice Writing in Cursive (Third and Fourth Grade)

Children's Books > Education & Reference > Words & Language

Children's Books > Education & Reference > Education > Workbooks

ISBN 10: 1468164643

EAN 13: 978-1468164640

Table of Contents

Introduction

The goal of this unique cursive handwriting workbook is to engage children and motivate learning through the use of creativity. Children enjoy reading wacky sentences like, "My teacher kissed a lizard." Exercises like these help to make learning fun, whether in the classroom or at home.

This Wacky Sentences Handwriting Workbook focuses on writing complete sentences in cursive. Students who need more practice writing individual letters or single words may benefit from using this workbook in combination with a basic cursive writing workbook which focuses on practicing letters and short words.

Four sections of this workbook help students develop their cursive writing skills at a variety of levels:

✓ Part 1 is for beginning writers. Students practice handwriting motions by tracing dotted sentences like, "Two rabbits slept on a fox's head."

✓ Part 2 advances to help students begin to write on their own. In this section, students first trace a dotted sentence and then copy the sentence onto a new line. The three traditional horizontal lines are included as a guide – solid top and bottom lines plus a dashed middle line help students master the relative heights of the letters, and to write across the page in straight lines.

✓ Part 3 gives solid sentences like, "Six elephants jumped over a giraffe," instead of dotted sentences like, "Six elephants jumped over a giraffe." At this stage, students practice their handwriting without first tracing the letters.

✓ Part 4 is the most advanced stage. The given sentences are now printed, like, "I put vanilla ice-cream on my pizza," and students must now rewrite them in cursive, like, "I put vanilla ice-cream on my pizza."

May your students or children improve their handwriting skills and enjoy reading and writing these wacky sentences.

Uppercase Cursive Alphabet

A B C D E F

G H I J K L

M N O P Q R

S T U V W X

Y Z

Lowercase Cursive Alphabet

a   b   c   d   e   f

g   h   i   j   k   l

m   n   o   p   q   r

s   t   u   v   w   x

y   z

Part 1 Trace Wacky Sentences

Part 1 Instructions: Trace directly over these dotted sentences.

Five monkeys got speeding
tickets for driving too fast.

I wore pajamas to school
and went to sleep in a suit.

A brave lion put his head
inside a man's mouth.

My little brother repeats
everything our parrot says.

The giraffe crawled under the

elephant to get his baseball.

Our principal likes to do

cartwheels in the hallway.

Two mice chased a cat who

tried to steal their cheese.

The spaghetti tasted like

gummy bears. Delicious!

My dog cooked dinner and

my cat washed the dishes.

In PE today, we played basketball on pogo sticks.

Fish held nets above the water to catch birds.

Quick turtles raced past the bunny rabbits.

Our bus driver picked us up in a tractor yesterday.

Just now it started to snow in our classroom.

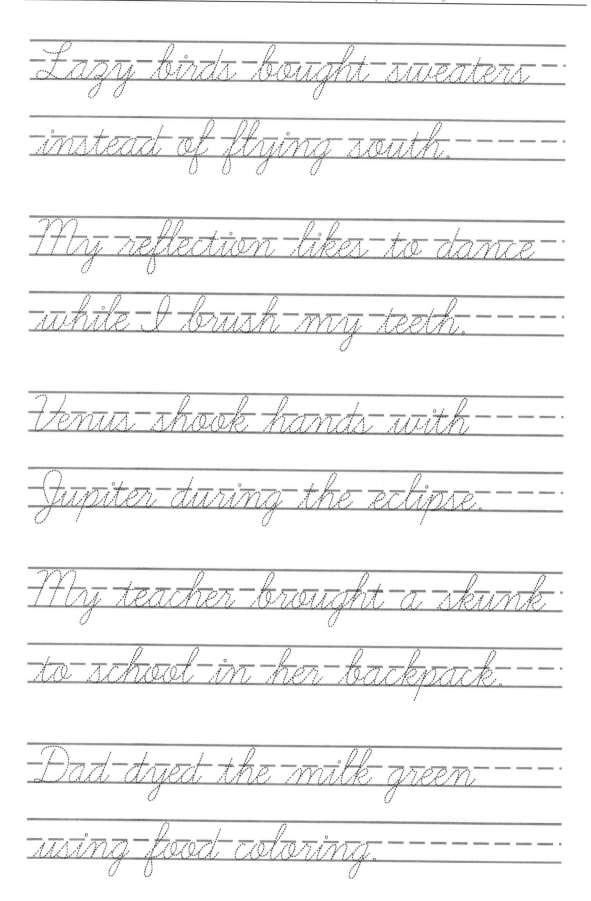

Lazy birds bought sweaters instead of flying south.

My reflection likes to dance while I brush my teeth.

Venus shook hands with Jupiter during the eclipse.

My teacher brought a skunk to school in her backpack.

Dad dyed the milk green using food coloring.

Six elephants jumped over a

giraffe using a trampoline.

A monkey got detention for

pretending to be a student.

An alien came to my house

to ask how to get to Mars.

Koala bears change the

lightbulbs at the ballpark.

The man in the moon

winked at me last night.

We kicked soccerballs at the
bowling alley on Friday.

Snowflakes floated up to the
clouds last Christmas.

What do you do when the
signal turns purple?

Her doctor gave himself a
shot to make her feel better.

The tooth fairy came down
the chimney on Halloween.

Most of the teachers wore
diapers on casual Friday.

Scuba divers sound funny
if they use helium tanks.

Rainbows must be sad
because they always frown.

Grandpa brought a goat in
my closet to eat the mess.

We like to play tennis with
skates and hockey sticks.

Penguins played dodgeball
with polar bears.

A hungry banana peeled an
orangutan during recess.

Have you ever seen an
alligator play hopscotch?

Zoo animals took a field
trip to our school last week.

My dog loves to wear jeans
on Sunday evening.

Checkers is hard when there
are three colors of squares.

Our vice principal sticks his
tongue out to say hello.

If we eat all of our cake,
we get chicken for dessert.

I waved to the Statue of
Liberty. She waved back!

The cow milked the farmer
first thing in the morning.

I don't walk my dog. We ride skateboards instead.

A damsel in shining armor saved a knight in distress.

Jumping beans are how our rabbit got stuck on the roof.

You should try playing kickball with clown shoes.

I ate my dog's homework to see how much he liked it.

The big bad piggy blew the
little wolf's house down.

We flew in a boat and then
rowed an airplane.

She brought a pet snake to
school to play jump rope.

Be nice to ghosts. They
might be afraid of people.

Eight monsters dressed up as
humans on Halloween.

Pizza flavored gum is better
than broccoli flavored cake.

A fish keeps a pet cat in a
tank full of air.

Pandas pushed my friend to
school in a red wagon.

Can you believe that our
teacher burps goodbye?

Unicorns use their horns to
play ping pong.

There is a raccoon living in

my locker at school.

Your principal likes to make

mud angels on rainy days.

We wear our clothes inside

out so they don't get dirty.

An ostrich sat on a football

and it hatched.

A baby changed my dad's

diaper on his birthday.

The angel wore a Christmas tree on her head.

A policeman tagged me and said I was it.

The sun stopped and changed direction. Was it lost?

There is a seal living in our pool who likes to play ball.

Would you like a cranberry popsicle or chocolate pickles?

We wore shorts on our

heads on wacky Wednesday.

An octopus was hiding in

my desk at school.

The only doors at my house

are on floors and ceilings.

His car has square tires and

walks like a lizard.

Four furry birds ran after

a cat that had feathers.

Part 2 Trace and Copy
Wacky Sentences

Part 2 Instructions: First trace directly over each dotted sentence, and then copy the sentence onto the blank lines below.

The fish swam across the

desert in one week.

I caught my grandparents

playing with my dolls.

A fine hydrant chased a dog.

There was a crawling band
at the parade.

Pigs and cows laughed. I
guess it was a funny farm.

Our teacher kissed a lizard.

My shadow went on
vacation today.

The airplane tiptoed across
the clouds to save fuel.

I woke my alarm clock up.

Some penguins were riding camels down the highway.

We got to dance on our desks during class yesterday.

My parents named me You.

It rained peanut butter and

jelly sandwiches last night.

Carrots were playing golf

with grapes on the counter.

The paper cut the scissors.

Students balanced fruit on
their heads during assembly.

Our up-side-down car has
wheels on its roof.

I was so sad, I laughed.

We had a screaming party at our library last month.

It only rained under my umbrella until I closed it.

I love to eat chocolate fries.

A galaxy tapped me on my shoulder to ask for the time.

A cat barked and a dog meowed, so we moved.

Trees skipped down the street.

Words words repeat repeat in in this this sentence sentence.

An artist drew a pencil with an eraser. Imagine that!

A whale played at the park.

We have carpet on the ceiling at our house.

My uncle lives in a nest in a very tall tree.

He sneezed through his ear!

When I bit a vampire, he
turned into a human being.

Santa Claus brought me
Easter eggs on Halloween.

The toilet burps as it flushes.

I laugh when I'm sad, but cry when I'm happy.

A matador charged at a bull that was holding a red cape.

A silly bear shaved his fur.

The parade featured an up-
side-down marching band.

All of the kids wore beards
and mustaches to class.

Ducks love spaghetti!

I put my pillow under my feet so they could sleep.

My teacher only thought I was late!

Deer wear chopsticks in May.

Five crows ate my corn for
lunch.

A porky pig and his cousin
ate my piggybank. Burp!

Grasshoppers are in my shoe.

I sleep under my bed so I
don't have to make it.

An elephant sat on my
desk and laughed.

Baby laughs, mommy cries.

Kiss a prince and you will marry a frog!

I rode a dinosaur to school, and he licked the nurse.

Elves ride zebras at night.

Mischief makers are looking for monkey business.

One gorilla sat on home plate eating a banana.

The moon wanted my cheese.

My puppy wears mommy's pants and shirts.

Daddy chews the doggie bone and barks. Arf arf...

A cat sleeps in a dog house.

The skunk wears toilet water perfume and 'before shave.'

Four fast turtles sped by the lazy sleeping dog.

Get hug from an octopus.

My teacher eats smores,

and then snores.

Chew gum while riding a

skating green elephant.

Dance when crickets chirp.

Alligators play baseball in
the snow on Mondays.

Laugh and sing while
the fish blow bubbles.

Lollipops tickled his armpits.

My camera takes pictures of itself. I take pictures of it.

The mailman puts postage stamps on his cheeks.

Kidney beans for breakfast!

Skunks love perfume and
long stemmed red roses.

When dad snores he rattles
the walls and windows.

My bird purrs like a kitten.

I can run backwards while juggling six ripe tomatoes.

Monster trucks with bicycle tires do wheelies in the dark.

I drive from the backseat.

A bear wants money to buy honey for his honey!

My piggybank ate all the bacon and hotdogs.

My cat growls like a dog.

I thought today was the day before tomorrow! Oh, it is!

Maybe so, maybe not. I really don't know. Do you?

I eat chocolate covered carrots.

Dancing on the moon three days in a row is hard work.

Giraffes came to town to party in the streets.

Onions cry, but we laugh.

I did my homework using invisible ink.

The computer mouse ran off with my cheese sandwich.

Wild cats love to party!

A chicken was born the day
my brother was hatched.

Two rabbits slept on a fox's
head.

Moons jump over cows.

Plain zebras chased striped lions.

A purple dog ran across the ceiling.

Part 3 Copy Wacky Sentences Without Tracing

Part 3 Instructions: Copy these sentences onto the blank lines. In this chapter, there is no tracing.

We balanced eggs on our

noses when we danced.

Smiley faces can't be

grumpy!

Clowns like pie wars.

I put vanilla ice-cream on

my pizza.

A horse with no name

danced on Main Street.

Kings love queens.

My parakeet flew off with the clock so time could fly.

Silly pirates wear clown makeup.

Girls giggle, jello jiggles!

Kids are baby goats. I'm a kid, but not a goat. I hope.

Jokers are wild and so am I. Sometimes, anyway.

I spy a bright flying saucer.

Funky flowered shoes are for dancing pink elephants.

The genius monkey is our teacher's pet.

Opossums hang around.

Vanilla ice-cream sprinkled with onions. Yummy!

Our bus driver missed the bus this morning.

My get-up-and-go just left.

Money grows on trees when locked in the bank vault.

Silly hyenas can't stop laughing.

Squirrels like to sky dive.

Bears go sledding on their bellies.

Ducks can waterski without skis.

Clowns wear funny makeup.

A big jack-o-lantern scared the black cat on Halloween.

Blue tongued zebras lick yellow lollipops.

Polar bears ski backwards.

Ski masks hide behind skiers.

Naughty elves need not apply.

My dog likes green noodles.

Cookies don't cry over spilt milk.

Vacuum cleaners pick up after my dirty feet.

Clowns wear bloomers.

Xerox machines mimic copycats.

Wet ducks swim in dry lakes on rainy days.

Bananas do the splits.

The space station doesn't
know which end is up.

Dumb questions get good
answers.

Astronauts are spacey.

Homework is fun when it is done.

Banjos were played by three rats nibbling cheese.

Useful tips give helpful hints.

Eager beavers were tardy
because they were too busy.

Our teacher likes no school
days.

Puzzles are puzzling.

My ten cents doesn't have

any sense.

Early birds get the worm

because no one wants it.

Music speakers can't speak.

The soda pop burped when I opened it.

Ghosts say boo when you scare them.

Mud hens need a bath.

My parakeet reads the

newspaper.

Skunks dream in black and

white.

Just forgot to remember.

Put some mojo in your

gas tank.

My sweet dreams scared

off the nightmares.

Pepperoni pizza has pizzazz!

Cool cucumbers are pickled
pink.

The hippopotamus wants to
be the biggest loser.

Gooney birds can't dance.

Zookeepers are locked up in cages every other Tuesday.

Zoo animals buy tickets to watch locked up zookeepers.

Dragon breath is fiery.

Our class took a field trip

to watch teachers.

Cold cocoa is served with

hot ice-cream on warm days.

Ice cubes make cool drinks.

Vegetables eat sassafras for dessert.

Dad parks his truck in the family room on Fridays.

Pack rats pack suitcases.

Xylophones are played by

sitting chimpanzees.

Tuna fish and cheerios are

yummy for my tummy.

My caterpillar is named Cat.

Green aliens like to scare

purple people.

Nine elephants play baseball

while our team eats peanuts.

Chocolate covered corn. Yum!

Quicksand ate my homework assignment.

Save your umbrella for a sunny day.

The comic read the funnies.

A blimp is a plane that ate too much.

The gorilla tried to fix the car using a monkey wrench.

Curly fries get perms.

On Halloween, I was so scary I scared myself.

Ants marched in the New Year's day parade.

Gooey gooey gumdrops!

Balloon racers need a lot of

hot air.

I met a yellow polka dotted

lady bug on Wednesday.

Astronomy goes forever.

We studied astronomy and I saw starlets.

Dragons can't win drag races dragging their tails.

Tasmanian devils are cute.

Tiny green men with funny ears visited our school.

School is cool when the air conditioner is working.

Part 4 Rewrite Printed Wacky Sentences in Cursive

Part 4 Instructions: Rewrite these sentences on the blank lines in cursive. Refer to pages 5 and 6 if you need help remembering what the cursive letters look like. Check your answers to Part 4 at the end of the book to make sure that you are practicing correctly. If you can fit the sentence on one line, write it twice.

The wolf turned into a man during the full moon.

Smart phones make the grade. Grade my phone please.

My German Shepherd barks in English.

Our brother howls at the full moon.

Sports drinks are sporty. Can you sport one for me?

Cows chew gum while people chew cud.

Chickens eat vegetable beef soup when they have a cold.

History is a class with a past and no future.

Math is a class with a lot of problems.

The bell broke so we didn't get a break today.

I painted an eye on my golf ball so I will always have my eye on the ball.

Dad takes our bird golfing so he'll always have a birdie.

On Thanksgiving, turkeys give thanks when we eat ham.

Mud hens eat mud pies.

Geese that tell jokes are silly geese.

If you sit on a cactus, it's a prickly situation.

My dog throws the ball, and I fetch it.

Mom put a tree in our house so I would have a tree house.

Sour grapes like to eat sweet candy.

I found my loss in the lost and found.

Blue cheese is found once in a blue moon.

Unicorns ride unicycles under ugly umbrellas.

Bear cats just grin and bear it.

Mechanics wearing monkey suits swing from the axles.

Knights in armor make shining examples.

Legoland is blocks of fun.

The principal expelled the camel for spitting.

Elephants carry their own showers.

A thousand snakes slithered over the skyscraper.

Hearts love valentines.   Give one to your heart on Valentine's day.

Is a duck-billed platypus a duck or what?

Can roadrunners go off-roading?

Dreams sleep so I can play.

Pigs speak Latin, but don't understand Pig Latin.

Wolves howl at the sun on Fridays.

Colorful parrots watch black and white TV.

Pancake syrup on pizza is delicious.

Hay, that's what horses dream about.

Cheerios are really cheery. Cheer up and have a bowl.

Meeting an eel can be very shocking.

Have you ever played darts with a stingray?

Sharks swim in my pool so I can swim in the ocean.

The ocean licks salt cubes.

My television watches me when I need a sitter.

We rode the double decker bus so we could have double scoop
ice-cream cones.

Pirates are gold diggers. Get it? They dig gold...

I sing to my radio. My radio listens.

Kites without tails fly upside down.

Santa gave me cookies and milk, and I gave him toys.

My parrot talks. I squawk.

You don't need a surfboard to surf the internet.

The biggest diamond is found on the baseball field.

Captain America eats hero sandwiches.

Why do willows weep? What made them so sad?

Mount Rushmore is very presidential.

Do snails get tired carrying their houses on their backs?

Turtles can hide in plain sight.

Horses sleep with their shoes on.

Kick boxing is a kick. Do you get a kick out of it?

Roller coasters can throw you for a loop.

Can we declare chocolate to be a vegetable?

My piggy bank ate my money and won't give it back.

I ate a square doughnut that didn't have a hole.

Are hula hoops for hula dancers?

Kangaroos have built-in pogo sticks.

Two purple bear cubs sled down the mountain on an orange toboggan.

Raccoons are masked bandits.

Dad says I can't play racquetball because I already make too much racket!

Dumbbells just weigh on you.

Lazy exercisers ride motorized bikes.

Half Dome is only half of what it could be.

The Grand Canyon is a very deep subject.

Life guards gave the trick-or-treaters life savers.

I forgot what I am supposed to remember.

Rodeo clowns are fun in a barrel.

What part of a drag race do drag racers drag?

Are ballpark franks only good at baseball games?

If you stretch a dollar bill, will it buy you more?

Dirt bike riders are really gritty.

Would the cookie monster still be a monster if he shared?

Why is it that all bobcats are named Bob?

Are goldfish really made of gold?

Wily roadrunners chase fast coyotes.

Clocks tell time, but you can't hear them.

Have you ever seen a giraffe on roller skates?

The elephant lent me his ear when I couldn't hear him whispering.

Yosemite Falls just keeps falling.

A wallaby is a kangaroo want-to-be.

Do jellyfish like strawberry jelly on their toast?

My dad likes peanut butter and jellyfish sandwiches.

Tennis shoes will only play basketball.

Do roadrunners ever walk?

Common sense only works when you think!

When you ice skate, you may start on your skates, but finish on your bottom.

A tow truck tried to tow our car while we towed a boat.

When golfing, the sand can really trap you.

Mixing red and blue ice-cream gives me a purple treat.

How big is a Super Bowl?

Have you ever seen a giraffe walk on stilts?

Do you have to do any other exercises during the seventh inning stretch?

Can a train help you keep your train of thought?

Our coach travels in a coach.

A temperamental camel got mad at the sphinx.

Women carry purses. Men carry wallets. Where do kangaroos carry their money?

It is great fun to hide my dad's TV remote.

I hide my mother's phone where she can't reach it, and then I call her.

The Painted Desert is very colorful.

Is the Oval Office really oval?

My dog gives me a treat if I speak on command!

Don't step on an elephant's toe because he'll never forget it.

Do race car drivers get dizzy after driving in a circle for three hours?

Can the Miami Dolphins swim?

When I wink at the stars, they wink back.

I ran so fast, my tennis shoe had a blowout!

Should the Badlands be punished?

Hot dogs aren't so hot.

Can you bend a rubber tree?

Could jumping beans jump higher if they weren't beans?

A roller skating giraffe could be a leg splitting experience!

Are sneakers really sneaky?

Carlsbad Caverns is a batty place.

Dodger dogs bark at ballpark franks.

Dirt biking is a really dirty sport.

Answers to Part 4

Page 84 :
Sentence 1.   The wolf turned into a man during the full moon.
Sentence 2.   Smart phones make the grade.   Grade my phone please.
Sentence 3.   My German Shepherd barks in English.

Page 85 :
Sentence 1.   Our brother howls at the full moon.
Sentence 2.   Sports drinks are sporty.   Can you sport one for me?
Sentence 3.   Cows chew gum while people chew cud.
Sentence 4.   Chickens eat vegetable beef soup when they have a cold.

Page 86 :
Sentence 1.   History is a class with a past and no future.
Sentence 2.   Math is a class with a lot of problems.
Sentence 3.   The bell broke so we didn't get a break today.
Sentence 4.   I painted an eye on my golf ball so I will always have my eye on the ball.

Page 87:

Sentence 1. Dad takes our bird golfing so he'll always have a birdie.

Sentence 2. On Thanksgiving, turkeys give thanks when we eat ham.

Sentence 3. Mud hens eat mud pies.

Sentence 4. Geese that tell jokes are silly geese.

Page 88:

Sentence 1. If you sit on a cactus, it's a prickly situation.

Sentence 2. My dog throws the ball, and I fetch it.

Sentence 3. Mom put a tree in our house so I would have a tree house.

Sentence 4. Sour grapes like to eat sweet candy.

Page 89:

Sentence 1. I found my loss in the lost and found.

Sentence 2. Blue cheese is found once in a blue moon.

Sentence 3. Unicorns ride unicycles under ugly umbrellas.

Sentence 4. Bear cats just grin and bear it.

Page 90:
Sentence 1. Mechanics wearing monkey suits swing from the axles.
Sentence 2. Knights in armor make shining examples.
Sentence 3. Legoland is blocks of fun.
Sentence 4. The principal expelled the camel for spitting.

Page 91:
Sentence 1. Elephants carry their own showers.
Sentence 2. A thousand snakes slithered over the skyscraper.
Sentence 3. Hearts love valentines. Give one to your heart on Valentine's Day.
Sentence 4. Is a duck-billed platypus a duck or what?

Page 92:
Sentence 1. Can roadrunners go off-roading?
Sentence 2. Dreams sleep so I can play.
Sentence 3. Pigs speak Latin, but don't understand Pig Latin.
Sentence 4. Wolves howl at the sun on Fridays.

Page 93:
Sentence 1. Colorful parrots watch black and white TV.
Sentence 2. Pancake syrup on pizza is delicious.
Sentence 3. Hay, that's what horses dream about.
Sentence 4. Cheerios are really cheery. Cheer up and have a bowl.

Page 94:

Sentence 1. Meeting an eel can be very shocking.

Sentence 2. Have you ever played darts with a stingray?

Sentence 3. Sharks swim in my pool so I can swim in the ocean.

Sentence 4. The ocean licks salt cubes.

Page 95:

Sentence 1. My television watches me when I need a sitter.

Sentence 2. We rode the double decker bus so we could have double scoop ice-cream cones.

Sentence 3. Pirates are gold diggers. Get it? They dig gold...

Sentence 4. I sing to my radio. My radio listens.

Page 96:

Sentence 1. Kites without tails fly upside down.

Sentence 2. Santa gave me cookies and milk, and I gave him toys.

Sentence 3. My parrot talks. I squawk.

Sentence 4. You don't need a surfboard to surf the internet.

Page 97:

Sentence 1. The biggest diamond is found on the baseball field.

Sentence 2. Captain America eats hero sandwiches.

Sentence 3. Why do willows weep? What made them so sad?

Sentence 4. Mount Rushmore is very presidential.

Page 98:

Sentence 1. Do snails get tired of carrying their houses on their backs?

Sentence 2. Turtles can hide in plain sight.

Sentence 3. Horses sleep with their shoes on.

Sentence 4. Kick boxing is a kick. Do you get a kick out of it?

Page 99:

Sentence 1. Roller coasters can throw you for a loop.

Sentence 2. Can we declare chocolate to be a vegetable?

Sentence 3. My piggy bank ate my money and won't give it back.

Sentence 4. I ate a square doughnut that didn't have a hole.

Page 100:

Sentence 1. Are hula hoops for hula dancers?

Sentence 2. Kangaroos have built-in pogo sticks.

Sentence 3. Two purple bear cubs sled down the mountain on an orange toboggan.

Sentence 4. Raccoons are masked bandits.

Page 101:

Sentence 1. Dad says I can't play racquetball because I already make too much racket!

Sentence 2. Dumbbells just weigh on you.

Sentence 3. Lazy exercisers ride motorized bikes.

Sentence 4. Half Dome is only half of what it could be.

Page 102:

Sentence 1. The Grand Canyon is a very deep subject.

Sentence 2. Life guards gave the trick-or-treaters life savers.

Sentence 3. I forgot what I am supposed to remember.

Sentence 4. Rodeo clowns are fun in a barrel.

Page 103:

Sentence 1. What part of a drag race do drag racers drag?

Sentence 2. Are ballpark franks only good at baseball games?

Sentence 3. If you stretch a dollar bill, will it buy you more?

Sentence 4. Dirt bike riders are really gritty.

Page 104:

Sentence 1. Would the cookie monster still be a monster if he shared?

Sentence 2. Why is it that all bobcats are named Bob?

Sentence 3. Are goldfish really made of gold?

Sentence 4. Wily roadrunners chase fast coyotes.

Page 105:

Sentence 1. Clocks tell time, but you can't hear them.

Sentence 2. Have you ever seen a giraffe on roller skates?

Sentence 3. The elephant lent me his ear when I couldn't hear him whispering.

Sentence 4. Yosemite Falls just keeps falling.

Page 106:

Sentence 1. A wallaby is a kangaroo want-to-be.

Sentence 2. Do jellyfish like strawberry jelly on their toast?

Sentence 3. My dad likes peanut butter and jellyfish sandwiches.

Sentence 4. Tennis shoes will only play basketball.

Page 107:

Sentence 1. Do roadrunners ever walk?

Sentence 2. Common sense only works when you think!

Sentence 3. When you ice skate, you may start on your skates, but finish on your bottom.

Sentence 4. A tow truck tried to tow our car while we towed a boat.

Page 108:

Sentence 1. When golfing, the sand can really trap you.

Sentence 2. Mixing red and blue ice-cream gives me a purple treat.

Sentence 3. How big is a Super Bowl?

Sentence 4. Have you ever seen a giraffe walk on stilts?

Page 109:

Sentence 1. Do you have to do any other exercises during the seventh inning stretch?

Sentence 2. Can a train help you keep your train of thought?

Sentence 3. Our coach travels in a coach.

Sentence 4. A temperamental camel got mad at the sphinx.

Page 110:

Sentence 1. Women carry purses. Men carry wallets. Where do kangaroos carry their money?

Sentence 2. It is great fun to hide my dad's TV remote.

Sentence 3. I hide my mother's phone where she can't reach it, and then I call her.

Sentence 4. The Painted Desert is very colorful.

Page 111:

Sentence 1. Is the Oval Office really oval?

Sentence 2. My dog gives me a treat if I speak on command!

Sentence 3. Don't step on an elephant's toe because he'll never forget it.

Sentence 4. Do race car drivers get dizzy after driving in a circle for three hours?

Page 112:

Sentence 1. Can the Miami Dolphins swim?

Sentence 2. When I wink at the stars, they wink back.

Sentence 3. I ran so fast, my tennis shoe had a blowout!

Sentence 4. Should the Badlands be punished?

Page 113:

Sentence 1. Hot dogs aren't so hot.

Sentence 2. Can you bend a rubber tree?

Sentence 3. Could jumping beans jump higher if they weren't beans?

Sentence 4. A roller skating giraffe could be a leg splitting experience!

Page 114 :

Sentence 1.   Are sneakers really sneaky?

Sentence 2.   Carlsbad Caverns is a batty place.

Sentence 3.   Dodger dogs bark at ballpark franks.

Sentence 4.   Dirt biking is a really dirty sport.

Workbooks by Julie Harper

✓ *Letters, Words, and Silly Phrases Handwriting Workbook (Reproducible): Practice Writing in Cursive (Second and Third Grade).*

✓ *Wacky Sentences Handwriting Workbook (Reproducible): Practice Writing in Cursive (Third and Fourth Grade).*

✓ Print Uppercase and Lowercase Letters, Words, and Silly Phrases: Kindergarten and First Grade Writing Practice Workbook (Reproducible).

✓ Print Wacky Sentences: First and Second Grade Writing Practice Workbook (Reproducible).

21455185R00067

Made in the USA
Lexington, KY
13 March 2013